REFLECTIONS

Rodney Charles Tuomi

ISBN 978-1-64258-904-7 (paperback)
ISBN 978-1-64258-905-4 (digital)

Christian Faith Publishing, Inc.
832 Park Avenue
Meadville, PA 16335
www.christianfaithpublishing.com

Printed in the United States of America

Hope Is Sprouting

Cold is growing old
Wind the snow does blow

May winter soon splinter
And wind chill take a pill

The days increase sun rays
From my chair to everywhere

Little green is now seen
Soon ground will be found

The Greatest Gift

Wrapped in old clothing
A mattress of soft straw
The crib a feed trough
Sent to fulfill God's law
Animals in attendance
Mighty angels deep in awe
The world paid little notice
God redeeming every flaw
Shepherds rejoicing
In worship at what they saw
Wise men needing to see Him
Bearing gifts coming from far
The greatest gift of Christmas
Jesus Christ, the Son of God

Ready for a January Thaw!

I enjoy all four seasons
Each having its own flavor

But this early sudden winter
Few have found to savor

Warmth and sun did abound
Then as a bully winter us found

Affecting all by an icy sudden blast
Many moons till we see green grass

Oh well, no more will I whine
An extra month shoveling will I labor

Winter . . . Gotta Love it!

Winter came early not going away
Invading fall and spring wanting to stay

I really do enjoy all four seasons
Each having its own special reasons

But this early sudden winter invasion
Few are found coming here to vacation

Warmth and sun did abound as I remember
Rudely winter pounced and it is only December

Affecting all by an icy sudden blast
All of us it has successfully harassed

Oh well a little less I will try to whine
Shoveling snow is just very fine…who am I kidding

A Simple Smile Will Do

Today I am busy
Going here and there

Hard to keep up
Having little time to care

So many people
Today that I meet

With a little extra effort
A smile others will greet

Little Furry Terrorists

Deciding to sit
In a small grove of oaks

Contemplating and dreaming
About God's love for all folks

My mind freewheeling
Actually half falling asleep

I heard these little thuds
Loud enough, making me leap

Then one plunked me
Right on the top of my head

Being bombed by acorns
Squirrel harassment, so I fled

Office Renovation

Sitting in my office
That is my chair by the beach

The walls are self-decorating
As nature's paintbrush does reach

Summer's green walls are changing
Spots of red, orange, and yellow

Places very bright and brilliant
Others soft and mellow

My air conditioner must be working well
A little cooler it seems today

Maybe I will start a fire
This office has a fire pit by the way

Enjoy the Parades

Throngs of people lining the streets
Kids scrambling for candy and treats

Fire trucks, police, and emergency lights
Sirens, many waving, and inspiring sights

Bands walking straight uniforms so neat
Loud music playing has us tapping to the beat

Floats, politicians, and other groups too
Standing in attention for the red, white, and blue

Many friends and people we know
Laughing, talking, and just letting go

Parades are special, a tradition of our land
Enjoying the people, fun, and every food stand

Thank you, Hibbing, and the other cities around
Parades gives us memories that forever abound

Hanging Out with the Loons

Sitting in my office by the lake
Listening to the loons lament
Hearing the hoot of an owl
Everywhere the croaking of frogs
Songs, chatters, and calls of many
Lapping waves washing my feet
Ambling clouds high above
Enjoying the scent of the breeze
Being warmed by bright sunshine

Hearing the loud hum of mosquitos
Brings me back to reality!

I Can Almost Smell the Flowers!

Enjoying the snow melting
Weather calling us to walks

Robins gleefully singing
Reconnecting with neighbors

Green slowly emerging
People starting to smile

Northerners loves spring more
Summer is knocking at the door

Take Time for Easter

The older I get, the larger the cross grows
As time passes, I realize that God only knows

So much I see not, little strength is really mine
Strength really comes by grace from His vine

God is so patient, will I ever learn
My goal is for Him to ever yearn

So many things in life continue to fade
The closer my walk with Him, less I am afraid

Spring Is Coming

Snails race
        Rocks erode
                Patience rules
        Spring is coming!

Choices

I slowly ambled down a path
Woodsy, winding, intriguing
Then came a place of decision
Two paths forked from the one
Which adventure should I follow
Do not choose too fast . . . ponder
Once one decides on a trail
It can become difficult to return
Creating a new way may get one lost
If I could just have past decisions back
I would choose my paths with greater
Care, prayer, and less dare

When It Is Done,
It Is Still Not Done

All the guests flew out the door
Only wrapping paper covers the floor
Being poor having bought out every store

So many of the gifts were just for frills
That will not change the amount of the bills
Our money fills many merchant tills

Some leftovers reek for maybe the next week
Cookies galore to keep me trim and sleek
In the fridge loving to peek, seek, and sneak

We love our Christmas lore and more
For this time of year is far from being a bore
Giving joy no matter what winter has us in for

Hope Is the Strength of Tomorrow

Dark clouds fill the skies
Strong winds sweep
A sliver of sunshine pierces
Brightness into our hearts leap

Peace is the fruit of yesterday

The Majestic Oak Tree

I paused to learn from a mighty oak tree
How many storms have you weathered
Were you ever almost blown down
How many droughts have you survived
Did thirst ever almost do you in
Have you ever survived a fire
Has a logger's ax ever come near
Numerous trees you must have birthed
Your acorns must have fed thousands
What have you seen in all your years
Surprising stories I believe you could tell
But you say so little
While your majesty speaks so much

I Can Already Taste It!

I can see it now on my plate
Turkey, dressing in amounts great

With mashed potatoes and gravy I have a date
Wanting seconds even though I just ate

For a dinner like that I am not late
As I write this, I cannot wait

Homemade pumpkin pie
With whipped cream piled high

Many friends stopping by
So many blessings . . . oh my!

But before I even start
Am I thankful to God deep in my heart
His blessings to us He wants to impart

(Psalm 100)

Dreams to Restore

The sun is shining
Warm is the day
      Leaves are colorful
      Gas in the tank
      All else can wait

Thoughts into me pour
Memories galore
New roads to explore
      The clock I ignore
      Should be done more

May God Bless You

My mind is blank
Into space I stare

I sit very still
With nothing to share

Thinking of others
I soon begin to care

So for you today
I send out a prayer

Friends

Problems here
Troubles there
Worries everywhere
Life can be a bear

Coffee with a friend
All is well 😊

My Favorite Church

Walking through the pines
Tall, straight, reverent

A floor of needles
A ceiling of boughs
A choir of birds
An altar of sunlight

Clouds like angels
Winds speaking truths

So simple
Yet
        So moving
      So spiritual
      So holy

The Beauty of Nature Enjoyed

Hope is the strength of tomorrow

Dark clouds fill the skies
Strong winds sweep
A sliver of sunshine pierces
Brightness into our hearts leap

Joy is the goal of today

Dawn gives its first hint
Birds erupt into song
Colorful sunsets paint the sky
Soon will stars the sky belong

Peace is the fruit of yesterday

God Bless You

A simple "God bless you"
Short and sweet
But what it says
Is beyond complete

For it asks
The God of all creation
Maker of heaven and earth
All-powerful
All-knowing
And ever present
His total grace bestowing
On every part of your life
Sheltering you in His arms
From now for evermore

Many Stories to Tell

A country church on a hill
    Faded white
    Windows boarded
    Grass long
All is still

I still hear the children
The dinners with much glee
Music, weddings, tears
Community was the key

What happened
Where did it go
It is so empty now
The strength of our past
May the spirit of life again blow

Freedom

Like chains wrapped around the soul
Hindering us from becoming whole

Unforgiveness never follows nor hides
But is our master as it in us resides

Thinking can become cruel and cold
And many of our decisions it will hold

Life is too short to be a slave to the past
Anything in life on God's grace can be cast

Silent Tears

Sometimes tears flow down our cheeks
Becoming rivers of the pain of life

Some emerge in reflection
Healing past issues and strife

Others erupt in joy
From laughter soothing our soul

But many are bottled inside to stay
Walking with us throughout every day

Enjoy

The grass turns brown
Then is white
      And finally it is green

Beauty hiding in the ground
Sprouts and can be seen

Much to do, and places to go
Life abounds and all is serene

He Is Risen

Love flowed through His eyes
As we nailed Him to the cross

He was beaten beyond recognition
But even deeper love came across

Blood puddled on the ground
His caring spirit endured the loss

Sacrifice beyond words bore all our sin
In a cold tomb His body they did toss

Rising from the dead defeated every foe
Let us remember the victory of the cross

Spring Does Have Its Issues!

Water running down the street
A welcome sight but gives me wet feet

Slush and melting are increasing more and more
But now the dog is tracking mud on the floor

Green will soon appear, putting winter in the rear
But that late heavy blizzard I do fear . . . oh dear!

Beauty

Your face humbles the beauty of the rose
Nature pauses, gazing as you pose

Life is full, and answers can be few
We often think . . . if I only knew

Learning to smell the roses helps joy grow
Some day we will see God and surely know

Icicles

Winter is aging
Melting grows

Melt, freeze, drip drip drip
Beautiful formations hang

Clear clean ice
Made brilliant by the sun

Toys for the young
Signs for the older

Rest in My Soul

Walking in the woods
The ground white with snow
Trees clothed with winter garb
Stillness, peace, and serenity grow
My body works, my mind rests
Cold winds refresh and cooling bestow
Something deep in me restores
Sunshine smiling on me below

Red and Green Everywhere Is Seen

Cookies baking fill the air
Lights and decorations everywhere
Special dinners shout for you I care

Choirs bless churches and schools
Time off . . . Christmas rules
Awaiting a yummy treat as it cools

Presents wrapped under the tree
People at worship on bended knee
Special times with our family

Born this season is the King of peace
May God's grace in our land increase
And the love of God from us release

Aimless Travel

A blanket of fresh snow
One set of footprints
Where do they go
Who made them
Is it someone I know
Maybe they are mine
As I wander to and fro

It Is Coming, Folks!

The weather is nice
People dread snow and ice

Oh no, it is going to snow
I hate winter; it is such a foe

But when all is covered in white
People love it so pretty and bright

Nature Painting

Dark clouds fill the sky
Showers from on high
Glints of sunshine pierce
Black skies look fierce
A colorful rainbow is nigh

Season's Change

Green, red, green here
Green, yellow, orange there
Brown, gold, brown everywhere
Soon the branches are bare

My Summer Friend

Summertime brings me a special friend

Sweet moments we have enjoyed
Chaos and drains of life often destroyed

Soon his leaving our fellowship will end
Chilly weather will him to another place send

Some go south during the cold
Others adjust and winter beauty behold

But my BBQ grill, my friend, the shed will soon tend

Gardens Galore

Blushing tomatoes plump with juice and taste
Yummy green peas like melons in the pod
Beans long and firm crowded on the bush
Cukes plump and topping many a salad
Carrots huge and orange looking like fall leaves
Onions bragging about their size and aroma
Pumpkins that could be used for a deer stand
Corn, cabbage, squash, spuds, and much more
Zucchini by the ton so lock your car door
Gardens reminding me of a grocery store
Lettuce enjoy every tasty bit to the very core

When Answers Are Few

Why doesn't God answer
Is there no solution to my prayer

My cries go up to Him
But into silence do I stare

Wait, have patience, I am told
Sometimes I wonder, does He care

What does God expect from me
Still waiting, but where do I go from there

The Fog Inside of Me

Fog blanketed the horizon and little was in sight
It was like viewing the distance in the dark of night

Everything moved slowly, and the world seemed still
Brisk was the summer morn having a touch of chill

But

Was it the fog that was really so intense
Or is it my mind that is just being very dense

On My Knees

Battles inevitably drive me to my knees
With tears and a cry to God pleading please

If I could just learn that my ability is so small
But God in His time and ways can do it all

Spending precious moments with my Lord
Makes my prayers a two-edged sword

The battles in life surely are many and fierce
But God's Spirit ultimately can any enemy pierce

My Friend the Pest

One night as I was falling into a deep sleep
I heard this buzz of a mosquito in flight

All of a sudden on my arm it did leap
I went from resting into a mode of fight

It was dark, so at it I slapped
I missed but incited it to strafe my head

Soon it landed on a spot on my ear it had mapped
So I whacked my ear wanting it dead

This went on for much time I knew
It would land, and I would swing

I just ended up black and blue
And off it went, I heard it sing

Sometimes we think that all is in control
When one small thing puts life on a roll

The Secrets of Life

A long walk
The sun is shining
All is green
    No bugs
Take your time . . . enjoy!

A Smile

A smile cost so little yet does so much
Even a stranger's life one can touch

The world is full of cold, empty stares
Smiling can show that one really cares

Smiles can light a fire in someone's heart
A mini miracle to a sad soul it can impart

Do I truly care for those that I meet
Warm smiles can heal pain and defeat

The Heavens at Night

Lightning flashes are a sudden bright light in the night
A spectacular sight dispersing some element of fright

The Lord shall return as the lightning from east to west
God's Word proclaims that truth and promise the best

His glory will be displayed along with His might
Looking for those who love Him will be His delight

Be ready

Spring Yard Work

My mind says go
My body says slow
My ambition says no
Always tomorrow although

Spring's Early Hello

Soon flowers will emerge from the ground
Bits of beauty here and there to be found
They cheer up one's day while driving around

I want to thank the many who plant a bed
So many colors, yellows, blues, greens, and red
They bless us without words being said

Just Enjoying Being Out

Here I sit out on the lake
Hoping for a few fish to take

I think the fish me do mock
My minnow is only taking a walk

My bobber just does not go down
Maybe I should go back to town

My son-in-law comes to the very same spot
And sends pictures of all the fish he just got

Helping Spring Along

Barbecuing in March
Jump starting spring
The aroma from the grill
Making my taste buds sing

Three Crosses

Three crosses on a hill
The center one eternal life to fulfill

One of the sides mocked and said no
The other cried for God's love to know

Which of the sides would be me
Choices decide our eternal destiny

A Hint of Spring

Walking in my beloved woods near the lake
Absorbing all of nature my senses can intake

The sun is starting to release its power
Snow banks are beginning to hide and cower

Tree branches are lifted up toward the sky
Awaiting a coat of green from on high

Spring is starting its muscle to stretch
Soon to chase winter to corner and catch

The Heavens at Night

The skies streaked with lightening is a light in the night
A spectacular sight dispersing some element of fright

Scripture says that He will return as the lightening East to West
The promises of God say it the best

His glory will be displayed along with His might
Looking for those who love Him will be His delight

Be Ready

"Watch therefore, for you do not know when the master of the house is coming--in the evening, at midnight, at the crowing of the rooster, or in the morning-- lest, coming suddenly, he find you sleeping. And what I say to you, I say to all: Watch!"
Mark 13:35-37

Nature's Quiet Time

A fresh blanket of fluffy snow
Enjoy it now for soon it will go

So pretty
       So white, so bright
             So clean, so serene
Nature at rest

A Poor Man's Vacation

Here I lay where it is so nice and warm
No bugs or mosquitos me to swarm

The temp varies little day or night
I'm so glad I came here; it feels just right

My eyes see no snow from where I lay
I may doze off for part of the day

Down south on some warm beach I am not
Just at home, reclining on my couch, is my lot

Blow, Blow, Blow Your Nose

A week or so ago, I picked up some bug
Actually, it was a big bad burly ugly thug

It felt like a truck was parked up in my nose
Wanting long-term storage to add to my woes

For a spell, my energy took a vacation
Seeming to have a one-way ticket to its destination

Bit by bit, my body has crawled back
Now to take inventory to see if I am intact

My Trusted Friend!

Winter so far this year has brought a smile, not a sob
But my snow shovel has been forced to take a second job

My shovel was even thinking about taking a vacation
But I insisted it stay for winter's duration

We have had little snow, and if it continues to refrain,
My shovel may have to take a refresher course itself to retrain

We do need some more snow, and the snowmen are few
2014 is over, and the year is brand new

Days are getting longer, and we are seeing more of the sun (hopefully)
Heating bills are lower, and winter is on the run (maybe)

The Heart of Christmas

Joy in the eyes of a child
Tears on a grandparent's cheek
A smile on a mom as people eat
Hugs from missed loved ones
Laughter the voice heard
A baby in a manger
The heart of Christmas

Christmas Cookies Baking

Standing by the oven, the aroma being so sweet
Waiting for hot cookies, a taste hard to beat

Sorry that this poem I will not complete
I see the treat, and it's time to eat!

Christmas Spirit

Packages wrapped under the tree
Of the many maybe one is for me

Nativity scenes housed in little stables
Fresh-baked cookies all over counters and tables

Colored outside lights proclaiming the season
Hoping my spending can stay within reason

Gathering with friends and people I know
Holiday wreaths adorned with a red bow

Children excited, carolers singing
Families united, bells a ringing

But the theme for Christmas really should be
Jesus was born for both you and me

Simple Joys

A fire lit
In the fire pit

Hot burning coals
Warms up my nose

A brat on a stick
Sizzling over glowing embers I pick

Hot juicy succulent flavor
With sweet aroma richly to savor

Contemplation

Walking along
On a clear crisp night

No moon out
Stars being the only light

Knowing each star has a story to tell
If I only knew

There is so much beyond me
Yet I can enjoy the view

Enjoy the Moment

Summer is gone
Fall is on the run
The days are getting chilly
There is a little less sun

No more mosquitoes
Nor dandelions to attack
But I think that I miss them
I want summer back

Peace

Sometimes I like to sit
Letting my mind unwind a bit

I love to do it by the shore
Oh, that I could do it more

Relaxation and peace
My energy they increase

A little calm in a world of unrest
The smile that emerges says it best

Autumn Beauty

I love reading nature's coloring book
So many trees call me to a second look

Soon they will fall

      red
            yellow
brown   orange
       gold

In me, the woods does now call!

God's Love

The smile of a baby
Love filling their eyes

Arms and legs moving excitedly
You being their prize

No words yet, maybe just a coo
Little they can do, but love they can be

That is how God yearns for us
Waiting from above on you and me

Nature's Call

I slowly rowed my boat along the shore
Stopping to listen and enjoy what nature had in store

Out on the lake several loons bobbing along
Laughter and lament came from their song

Soothing . . . eerie . . . joyful . . . and strong

A deep message resonated, full of wild lore
I just sat and listened, waiting for more

Reflections

The all-class reunion was truly a great week
My class get-together was a time into the past to peek

After seeing and talking with many old friends
I gazed through my 1969 yearbook to reflect on memories it lends
So many reminders, thoughts, and riches my Hematite sends

Paging through, the changes amazed me in so many people I knew
Until I looked at my own picture—oh my, case dismissed, whew
Changes in myself are more than a few

All-Class Reunion

Many faces, lots of smiles
Tired feet, too many miles

Tons of memories, stories galore
Even being tired, one wants more

Eating here, eating there
Much laughter, not a care

So many people I remember so well
If I could recall their names, that would be swell

One Step at a Time

The sun is shining, the grass is green, the sky is blue
It seems easy to surf on top of the waves of life

But other days are gray, in the sky, and inside us
And little issues have us wrestling with strife

Sometimes we can look ahead, expecting what is good
Other times the past is like an anchor dragging behind

But God's grace never changes
If we can just take one day at a time

Summer Breeze

The other day, my dog took me on a lengthy walk
We ended up walking many a block

He snooped and sniffed at everything in sight
Like one at garage sales meandering with delight

As we journeyed, his nose went up and twitched in the air
I suspect that he smelled a barbecue somewhere out there

After a slow and enjoyable cruise
He settled down for a long afternoon snooze

Dandelions

The time to cut the lawn has come
Hopefully, my mower will not sputter but hum

It usually takes me less than an hour
To mow the grass and dandelions, my favorite flower

As I bore down, those dandelions were golden and grinning
I fear there is some sinister plot that they are spinning

Finally, when I finished mowing the grass,
I looked around to see several yellow dandies already up laughing
with a sass

Nature's Tweet

Darkness and mystery fill the night
Stillness and quiet walk the ground

It is broken by a slight hint of light
Then an eruption of song from the trees is found

A choir of birds floods the air with joy
Announcing the day while it is still away

It is a time to stop, listen, and enjoy
The concert is brief and then goes away

The Cross

The cross, so simple, so plain
It bore my Lord, His torment, His pain

He had a choice, the cross or not
But our forgiveness His blood bought

Our sins are many and oh so black
He became sin and died to bring us back

We don't see our sin, being so blind
His love gave His life to redeem mankind

Camping

Raindrops softly falling, relaxing you to sleep
So much better than trying to count sheep

Bacon frying in the pan, the most wonderful alarm
A hot cup of coffee in the crisp air captures life's charm

The wind speaking through the pines, a natural sedative
We must rest and relax to fully learn how to live

A warm comfy crackling fire, your focus for hours
Deep communication without words, much stress devours

Camping

Determined to stay camping until I catch a fish
Stay here long enough may give me my wish

Raindrops still softly falling relaxing you to sleep
All that fresh air allows you to sleep so deep

Bacon frying in the pan still the most wonderful smell
A hot cup of coffee in the wild and all is well

Still catching nary a fish even one would be my wish
Trying every possible bait wanting fresh fish in my dish

Ducks quacking in the lake nature's sedative
Resting and relaxing soaking up what nature has to give

A warm comfy crackling fire just never ever gets old
Deep communication with myself being warm in the cold

Still no fish but no anguish since in all else I have bliss

Soon

Soon for the summer winter will hibernate
And hopefully may God summer liberate

The cold and snow may frustrate
But a gorgeous summer would compensate

May the leaves on the trees soon ornate
And may no late blizzards complicate

A long lovely warm spring would be great
Soon the fish will be nibbling on our bait

Relaxation

Hobbies are a joy and delight in life
We need time frames that reduce our strife

Relaxation can be a mini vacation
Allowing our being some recreation

Energy and strength need to be released
And problems of life seem to be decreased

I've had many joys in life that come and go
But my latest pursuit seems to be shoveling snow

The Chickadee

Gray and white
With a cap of black
A bird of little might
One inch through from front to back

Wind chills of forty below
Yet this bird winter survives
Does God on His creatures care bestow
That is proof plenty that God is alive

Warmth

Dear Lord, please hear my prayer
Could you add more heat into the air

Winter has been cold and a little long
I'm not complaining, so don't get me wrong

We are looking for spring soon one day
Please not like last year when it came in May

Thank you, Lord, for listening to me whine
Warm weather in March would be just fine

Winter Needs to Chill a Little

The attitude of this winter is bold
Forecasts call for continued cold
This is starting to get a little old

We desire more blue sky
As the sun climbs higher in the sky
Warm weather has been kinda shy

Winter has had quite a run
Soon the cold will be done
Please warm up and let us have fun

Christmas Gatherings

A room full of friends
Conversation so warm to the day lends

Fresh cut balsam a sweet smell sends
Decorations and flowers to the season blends

Gifts sending messages that never ends
The attitude of the heart to God bends

Love exchanged to life's pain amends
The joys giving us strength that defends

He Is Born

And she brought forth her firstborn Son and wrapped Him in swaddling clothes and laid Him in a manger, because there was no room for them in the inn. Now there were in the same country shepherds living out in the fields, keeping watch over their flocks by night. And behold, an angel of the Lord stood before them, and the glory of the Lord shone around them, and they were greatly afraid.

Then the angel said to them, "Do not be afraid, for behold, I bring you good tidings of great joy which shall be to all people. For there is born to you this day in the city of David a Savior, who is Christ the Lord."

After Jesus was born in Bethlehem of Judea in the days of Herod the king, behold, wise men from the East came to Jerusalem, saying, "Where is He who has been born King of the Jews? For we have seen His star in the east and have come to worship Him."

And when they had come into the house, they saw the young Child with Mary, His mother, and fell down and worshipped Him. And when they had opened their treasures, they presented gifts to Him: gold, frankincense, and myrrh.

In the beginning was the Word, and the Word was with God, and the Word was God. In Him was life, and the life was the life of men. And the Light shines in the darkness, and the darkness does not comprehend it. And the Word became flesh and dwelt among us, and we beheld His glory, the glory as of the only begotten of the Father, full of grace and truth.

Jesus was born. Jesus walked on earth as a sinless sacrifice. Jesus died for our sins. He is in glory now, and He is coming again. How can we not celebrate Christmas by first loving Him and then loving and remembering each other! Put the Savior first this season, and then celebrate with festive meals, great fellowship, family gatherings, exchanging presents, being generous to the poor, spending time in prayer, and loving one another!

An angel was the first one to preach Jesus after He was born. The shepherds were the first ones to worship Him after He was born, and the wise men were the first ones to give Christmas gifts to Him after He was born. I want to fall in line with all three in my Christmas celebration. Merry Christmas! Let us worship together!

I love the smell of balsam cut fresh from the trees
But I love more to worship my Jesus down on bended knees

I enjoy the bounty of food so savory and appealing
But only after a time of weeping in prayer while I am kneeling

Bring on the reds and greens of the season
Keeping in mind that Jesus birth is the reason

Singing Christmas hymns and songs of praise
With a heart full of joy and a hand I do raise

Worshipping God and pouring love into people
Knowing that we are God's church with its cross and its steeple

Missing Camping Already

The smell of bacon sizzling in the pan
Brewing coffee steaming and calling
A faint sniff of wood smoke part of the plan
Camping have to wait till the snow stops falling

The Holidays Are Coming

The fragrant smell of roasting turkey fills the house
Maybe with a chicken or possibly some grouse

Hams bake bathing and bubbling in their juice
Their inviting aroma wandering out on the loose

Rivers of gravy flow, begging to join the feast
Flooding the mashed potatoes at the very least

Special ethnic delights served with pride and joy
Appearing to paint memories and taste buds to employ

Fresh-baked pies lining the counter ready to meet their fate
The lingering smell a memory to contemplate

Cookies of all sorts, so inviting and yummy
Looking to be adopted and find a home in a tummy

The smiles, laughter, love, and the friendship so warm
Blessings from God over us really do swarm

Being Thankful

Sometimes life seems so gray
And hope seems all but gone
Some people live in this every day
And for a bit of joy do long

Thanksgiving is more than a thought
But an attitude deep in our soul
Being grateful gives the answers sought
And makes life more healthy and whole

Collecting Ones Thoughts

A warm evening
The moon is full
Enjoying a long walk

Listening to nature sing
Feeling the need for quiet pull
With the inner self having an long talk

Seasons Change

The sun seems to be sleeping in a little later
And going to bed earlier than before
Autumn colors will soon proclaim the Creator
As fall is gently knocking at the door

Summer did appear and smile brightly
Though its smile's stay was not very long
We pack in so much day and nightly
Because fall will soon be singing its song

One Day at a Time

Pain comes in many sizes, shapes, and forms,
It paves the pathways of our life
Often it is the black in the clouds of our storms,
Creating internal turmoil and strife
Look up, look up, our help comes from on high,
But often the pain does not go away
For help and deliverance we loudly cry,
But the answer usually is strength for another day

Nature's Therapy

Relaxing by the shore,
The sunshine set on bake
Eyes closed to enjoy,
The lapping of waves off the lake

A moment of rest,
Needed time for the soul to take

The world at peace,
At least a moment for my sake

Old Glory

I salute the Red
                White,
                              And Blue,
To my country I am true

We have stood for truth and opposed the wrong,
Sacrifice and toil have made this country strong

Many have tried to defeat this great land,
But we are upheld by God's mighty hand

The only way we can become weak
Is if our God we fail to seek

Finally Fishin'

No snow
No ice
Open water
Oh so nice!

Grass

Brown
Green
    Mow

Strength in a Smile

The sun shining bright
      A smile so warm
Gives body and soul light
      And can still the storm
Routine can wear
      Energy can fade
A little kindness and care
      And new strength is made

The Joy of Quiet

The moon so bright, so full, so round
      Its soft glow a carpet to the ground
Giving us light to explore each sound
      Creation so simple yet so profound
Peace during the quiet has again been found
      A chance for my soul to become unwound

Longing and Ready

I do miss the green,
For a season it has been unseen.
Even if I need to mow,
My grin will continue to grow.
Lord, I promise not to complain,
Instead of snow, I want to see rain.

Northern Lights

Dancing on the northern sky
     All of heaven being their stage.
Reaching to worship God on high
     Colors erupt, and colors fade.
At times they ebb, at times they flow
     Sometimes soft and sometimes bright,
Bringing to the darkness a heavenly glow
     Entertainment late at night.

Spring

Watching the snow melt
Makes spring heartfelt.
Enjoying the sunshine
Seems to make the day go fine.
Seeing the water run
Sniffs at summer fun.
Still wanting to enjoy the snow,
Enjoy each day that we are given here below.

Hope

Dawn's first light
                The day is new.
Hope is bright
                The sky is blue.

The grace of God
            So pure and clean.
Through life we plod
            Love's face is seen.

We Need You Every Hour

A small rural town
An old white church

Snow on the steps
Why is it not shoveled

Paint peeling off the door
Does no one care

No one sitting in the pews
We should need more churches

But the steeple's pointing to high
Our God is the source of life

About the Author

Rodney Charles Tuomi was born in the small Northern Minnesota city of Hibbing, located about one hundred miles from the Canadian border.

He was a good student and was active in many school activities. He also spent much time at the family cabin located on a lake near Hibbing. He also enjoyed spending times in the woods and at other lake areas.

His mother grew up in a farming town in North Central Minnesota, and much time was also spent at the farm. His mother's family was very large and very close, and numerous holidays and get-togethers were spent at the farm or at the cabin.

He also spent parts of many summers growing up helping and working on his uncle's farm. His father was a carpenter in the iron ore mines in the Hibbing area and was an outdoorsman with a deep love for nature, trees, lakes, and being in the wild. Rodney developed a deep love for family, nature, animals, and being outdoors.

Rodney also has a love for science and has several engineering degrees. He graduated from the University of Minnesota in 1973 with a BS in chemical engineering. He is deeply devoted to God, having developed a relationship with his Lord at an early age. He worked as an engineer for a season but was also active in many areas of church and community ministry. He pursued additional studies.

He went full-time into the ministry in 1980, being ordained a few years later. Though through the years he has worked some as an engineer, his love has always been the church and has been active in pastoral ministry for many years.

He is currently the senior pastor at a small church in Hibbing, where he has been active in ministry for twenty-three years. He loves people, loves nature, and has been active as an engineer, a pastor, a counselor, a community leader, and an author. After writing for many years, God has been calling more and more in his life to write. He is a father of four and a grandfather of three. His children and grandchildren are the joy of his life. This is the first book that he has written.

CPSIA information can be obtained
at www.ICGtesting.com
Printed in the USA
BVHW041132270423
663151BV00007B/330